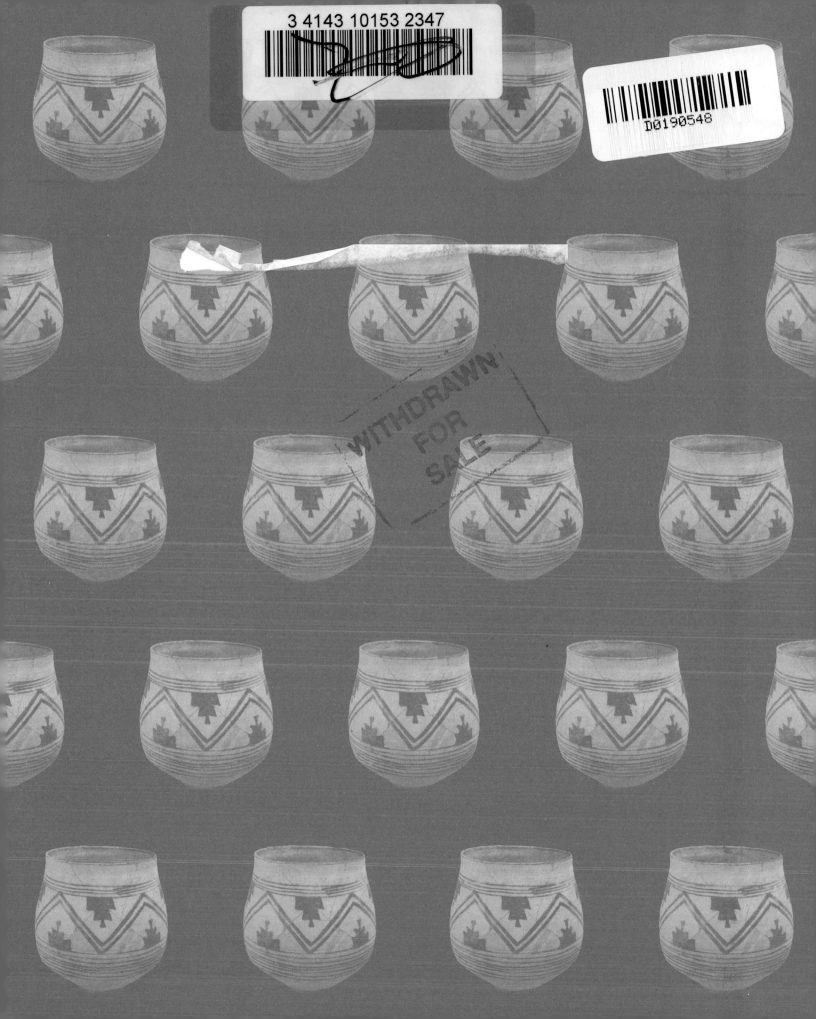

THE INDUS VALLEY

THE HISTORY DETECTIVE INVESTIGATES

Claudia Martin

WAYLAND

First published in 2014 by Wayland

Wayland
338 Euston Road
London NW1 3BH

Wayland Australia
Level 17/207 Kent Street
Sydney, NSW 2000

The History Detective Investigates series:

Produced for Wayland by
White-Thomson Publishing Ltd
www.wtpub.co.uk
+44 (0)843 208 7460

Editor: Claudia Martin
Designer: Alix Wood
Consultant: Philip Parker
Proofreader: Lucy Ross
Cover concept design: Lisa Peacock

A catalogue record for this title is available from the British Library.

ISBN: 978-0-7502-8437-0
eBook ISBN: 978-0-7502-8539-1

Dewey Number: 934.9'1-dc23

Printed in Malaysia

10 9 8 7 6 5 4 3 2 1

Wayland is a division of Hachette Children's Books, an Hachette UK company

Picture Acknowledgments: Afsar Husain/Ancient Art & Architecture Collection: 12, 24; **British Museum:** 9l; **Brooklyn Museum:** 17l; **Stefan Chabluk:** 5t, 20; **Comrogues:** 11b; **Corbis:** cover bottom (Ursula Gahwiler/Robert Harding), 13 (Angelo Hornak), 15t (Alfredo Dagli Orti/The Art Archive), 15b (Robert Harding), 23t (Angelo Hornak); **Daderot/Royal Ontario Museum:** 14, 19b; **Dreamstime.com:** 7t (Digikluk), 11t (Jerry Rainey), 16 (Attila Jandi), 19t (Gauravmasand), 21b (Dr Pramod Bansode), 23b (David Porter), 27b (Samrat35), 29t (Antonella865); **DVIDSHUB:** 27t; **Getty Images/UIG:** 22; **Grjatoi:** 8; **Himalyan:** 7b; **Ismoon:** 1, 25, 28 (National Museum, New Delhi), 2 (CSMVS, Mumbai); **National Museum, New Delhi:** 18; **Obed Suhail:** 29b; **Shutterstock:** cover top (vlad0209), 4 (Szefei); **SuperStock/Robert Harding:** 5b, 6, 10, 17r, 21t; **Werner Foreman/Edgar Knobloch:** 9r, 26.

Above: This is a mould taken from an Indus Valley seal. It shows a human figure between two tigers.

Previous page: This figurine of a woman was made in the Indus Valley between 2600 and 2000 BCE.

Cover top: The Indus Valley in modern-day Pakistan.

Cover bottom: The Citadel at Mohenjo-Daro.

CONTENTS

Words in **bold** can be found in the glossary on page 30.

The history detective Sherlock Bones will help you to find clues and collect evidence about the Indus Valley. Wherever you see one of Sherlock's paw-prints, you will find a mystery to solve. The answers are on page 31.

WHEN WAS THE INDUS VALLEY CIVILIZATION?

Between around 3200 BCE and 1700 BCE, a civilization flourished around the River Indus and its tributaries, which flow through modern Pakistan and India. The people of this civilization lived in great cities and crafted beautiful objects. Their civilization covered around 1 million sq km (400,000 sq mi), making it four times the size of the United Kingdom.

Like all early peoples, at first the Indus Valley people were hunter-gatherers: they lived by gathering wild plants and hunting animals to eat. Around 6500 BCE, some Indus Valley people began to learn how to grow crops and keep animals, so they settled down to become farmers. Over time, villages and towns grew up. By around 2600 BCE, Indus Valley people were building large cities, such as the two that **archaeologists** have named Mohenjo-Daro and Harappa.

Although archaeologists have named the Indus Valley **civilization** after one river, the Indus, the cities and towns were actually clustered in two **river basins**: the Indus and Ghaggar-Hakra. Without these rivers, there would have been no civilization.

DETECTIVE WORK

Discover what types of objects have been found in the Indus Valley by using the Metropolitan Museum of Art's website: http://www.metmuseum.org. Type Indus Valley into the 'Search' box.

The River Indus has its source on the high Tibetan Plateau. It flows 3,180 km (1,980 mi) through India and Pakistan before emptying into the Arabian Sea.

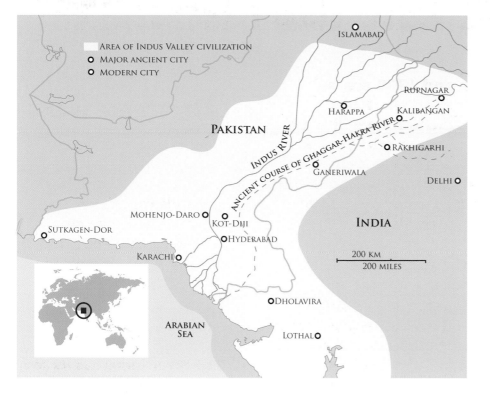

AREA OF INDUS VALLEY CIVILIZATION
○ MAJOR ANCIENT CITY
○ MODERN CITY

ISLAMABAD

RURNAGAR
HARAPPA KALIBANGAN
PAKISTAN INDUS RIVER
ANCIENT COURSE OF GHAGGAR-HAKRA RIVER
RAKHIGARHI
GANERIWALA
DELHI ○
MOHENJO-DARO ○
KOT-DIJI
○HYDERABAD INDIA
SUTKAGEN-DOR ○
KARACHI ○
200 KM
200 MILES
○DHOLAVIRA
ARABIAN
SEA LOTHAL○

The Indus Valley civilization was at its largest between around 2600 BCE and 1900 BCE. Its major cities were in the valleys of the Indus and Ghaggar-Hakra Rivers.

This statue of a woman was made in Mohenjo-Daro.

The rivers carried **nutrients** down from the mountains in **silt**. In the rainy season, the rivers overflowed, drenching the valleys with nutrients that made the soil perfect for farming. As Indus people became skilled farmers, the rich soil and plentiful water gave them more food than they needed. The rivers also offered fish to catch. Now not everyone needed to work at finding food: they could specialize in house-building or making goods from clay. These craftspeople traded their goods with the farmers for food.

When Indus Valley people started to build cities, they kept them close to the rivers, where there was water for drinking, cooking and washing. The rivers were also useful for transporting the goods that the craftspeople were making. Many archaeologists believe that the rivers were so important to Indus Valley people that water became central to their religion.

🐾 **What do you think this small statue might have been made from?**

OW DO WE KNOW ABOUT THE INDUS CIVILIZATION?

By 1700 BCE, most of the Indus Valley cities had been abandoned. They were slowly covered by soil and vegetation – and were almost forgotten. But local people still told stories about the ancient cities. In the nineteenth century, archaeologists started to unearth them.

The first archaeologist to **excavate** in the Indus Valley was Sir Alexander Cunningham (1814–93). Between 1853 and 1872, he discovered tools and pottery while digging at Harappa. But what most interested him was a stone **seal**. Over 3,700 of these ancient seals were later found in the Indus Valley.

Most seals are about 2.75 cm (1 in) square, with a hole at the back that could have fitted a cord. They were carved from a soft stone called soapstone, using chisels and drills, then baked in a kiln to harden them. Although some seals show people or gods, most show an animal along with some symbols, which are likely to be a form of writing. Particular animals, such as unicorns and water buffalo, are shown again and again.

The archaeologist Sir John Marshall (1876–1958) was the first to realize that the Indus Valley was the site of a great civilization. In 1924, he wrote in a magazine:

'Not often has it been given to archaeologists… to light upon the remains of a long-forgotten civilization. It looks, however, at this moment, as if we were on the threshold of such a discovery in the plains of Indus.'

The earliest seals date back to 2600 BCE. This one shows a unicorn-like animal standing in front of what may be a brazier for burning incense.

🐾 **Which animal is most commonly seen on Indus Valley seals?**

Archaeologists believe that the seals were used as stamps: they were probably pressed into soft clay to show the ownership of goods. Perhaps they were worn around the necks of traders and craftspeople, like modern identity cards. It is possible that the different animals represent different groups of tradesmen. The high number of seals tells us something very important about the Indus Valley: trade was vital to the people of the region.

The seals also highlight something that we are still trying to find out about the valley. The earliest writing found there is on seals. Unfortunately, no one has yet **deciphered** this script, because we have nothing to compare it with to help us translate. So far, around 420 different symbols have been seen on seals and other objects. This is too many symbols for them to represent an alphabet. Perhaps the symbols represent syllables or perhaps they stand for whole words. The symbols most often seen on seals are fish and jars, which seems to make sense for traders living beside fish-filled rivers.

Archaeologists dig carefully in the soil to unearth the remains of ancient civilizations, from houses and pottery to skeletons.

DETECTIVE WORK

Use this website to find out exactly what archaeologists do and what tools they use: http://archaeology.mrdonn.org

The city of Dholavira is one of the most recent Indus Valley cities to be discovered. Excavations started in 1990.

WHICH INDUS VALLEY CITY WAS THE BIGGEST?

The largest city excavated in the Indus Valley is Mohenjo-Daro. It had a population of perhaps 40,000 people and covered an area of up to 2 sq km (0.8 sq mi). Over 1,000 other cities, towns and villages have also been found. At its height, the Indus Valley civilization was probably home to around 5 million people.

Archaeologists have discovered that Mohenjo-Daro was split into two parts. To the west was the walled **Citadel**, which some archaeologists believe was the site of the government and other important buildings. To the east was the Lower City, where the ordinary people lived and worked. The Citadel was built on a brick platform 12 m (39 ft) above the Lower City. This gave it protection from the river's floods and enemy attack.

Several large buildings have been excavated in the Citadel. Archaeologists have named one of them the Great Bath. In the middle of the building is what seems to have been a pool, 7 m (22 ft) wide, 12 m (39 ft) long and 2.5 m (8 ft) deep. It must have been a public bath or swimming pool, but its central location has made archaeologists wonder if it was used for religious ceremonies based around water.

In 1842, a traveller in the region, Charles Masson, wrote about legends of the lost city of Harappa:

'Tradition [tells us about] the existence here of a city, so considerable that it extended to Chicha Watni, thirteen cosses [42 km; 26 mi] distant.'

The Great Bath is in the foreground of this photo of Mohenjo-Daro. The circular building is a Buddhist shrine that was built long after the city was abandoned.

Next to the Great Bath is a building that early archaeologists thought was a **granary**, as it was built on blocks to help air flow underneath and perhaps keep a grain store fresh. However, no grain has been found there, so perhaps this huge building was actually a palace or a temple. Close to the Granary is a square, pillared structure that has been called the Pillared Hall. It may have been used as a meeting hall.

The Lower City of Mohenjo-Daro was built on a regular street plan. Blocks of houses were divided by a grid of narrow alleyways and wider main streets, up to 11 m (36 ft) across. Mohenjo-Daro was way ahead of its time when it came to its water supply and drains. In fact, the Indus cities were the world's first to have **sewer** systems. Fresh water was supplied to the city's inhabitants through countless public wells, while many larger homes had private wells. Drains ran from most of the city's houses to carry away waste water, feeding into sewers that ran underneath the streets.

DETECTIVE WORK

To take a closer look at the Indus Valley cities, explore http://www.harappa.com. The website is put together by archaeologists from around the world.

A paved alleyway runs between homes in the Lower City.

| 0 | 10 | 20 | 30 m |
| 0 | 25 | 50 | 75 ft |

This plan shows a section of the Lower City of Mohenjo-Daro. Homes and workshops of different sizes can be seen.

Which direction did Mohenjo-Daro's main streets run: north–south or east–west?

HOW WERE THE CITIES BUILT?

The people who designed the Indus Valley cities were very skilled: they knew how to make complex structures such as sewer systems and wells. The construction work itself must have been done by hundreds of brickmakers, bricklayers and carpenters.

Before building work began on cities such as Mohenjo-Daro and Harappa, they must have been carefully planned out: the street grid and sewer plan were designed so that all waste flowed out of the city. This makes these cities different from those of other civilizations of the period, which grew up in a much less ordered manner. All this planning must have been done by people with jobs something like modern **architects** and **engineers**. They knew how to build **reservoirs** and brick-lined wells, up to 20 m (65 ft) deep, which could collect rainwater without collapsing from the pressure. In order to make wells, drains and the Great Bath watertight, they lined them with **bitumen** tar, sandwiched between two layers of brick.

Archaeologists have found some building tools that may have been used in the construction of the cities: flint blades, drills and scrapers; bronze axes, chisels and knives; and copper saws. Some of the world's earliest rulers, made from ivory and dating back to 1800 BCE, have been unearthed in Indus Valley sites. They might have been used to measure bricks and other building materials.

In the 1940s, the archaeologist Sir Mortimer Wheeler carried out excavations in the Indus Valley. He wrote:

'The high quality of the sanitary arrangements at Mohenjo-Daro could well be envied in many parts of the world today.'

The brick-lined drains of Mohenjo-Daro ran into underground sewers that travelled down the centre of the streets.

Drain

Sewer

Why were sewers often covered with removeable stone slabs?

In some parts of the world, mud bricks are still made by the same method used in the Indus Valley 5,000 years ago.

Stone was in short supply locally, so the early Indus Valley settlements were built with mud bricks. The brickmakers mixed clay and soil with water, then pressed it into a wooden brick-shaped mould. The bricks were turned out to dry in the sun. By the time they were constructing the great Indus Valley cities, the builders had learnt that bricks baked in a kiln last longer than sun-dried bricks and are less affected by water. For this reason, baked bricks were used for lower walls, sewer systems and wells, while the upper walls were usually built with sun-dried bricks, which are cooler in hot weather.

All the bricks used in Indus Valley cities had the same dimensions. Although they were in different sizes, with larger bricks used in city walls than in houses, the bricks were always made in the ratio of 4:2:1. Their length was double their width, which was double their depth. The walls of cities were also of a standard size and shape. Someone, or a group of people, must have laid down rules about the style and standards of building right across the civilization.

DETECTIVE WORK

Take a tour of Mohenjo-Daro for a closer look at how the city's streets, drains and buildings were constructed: http://www.mohenjodaro.net/. How many people do you think it took to build one house?

Bricks were slotted together in a bond pattern that has in some cases lasted to this day. Timber was used to strengthen certain walls, but the wood rotted away long ago.

WHO RULED THE INDUS VALLEY?

Sometimes the things that archaeologists do not find are as interesting as the things that they do find. So far, no one has found a richly decorated royal palace or a monument to an important person in the Indus Valley. But we can still do some detective work about who ruled the valley.

The 'priest-king' statue is 17.5 cm (7 in) tall. The cloak was originally painted red.

We know about the pharaohs who ruled ancient Egypt because of the great monuments they built, and the written records that have survived. We have neither of these things to help us discover who ruled the Indus Valley. However, archaeologists can make some guesses about the valley's rulers. They base their guesses on the evidence they have found and on the ways in which other civilizations of the period were ruled.

In 1927, archaeologists discovered a small statue of a man in Mohenjo-Daro. It was lying in a building with unusually fancy brickwork. Unlike most statues discovered in the valley, it is made from stone rather than clay. This suggests it was intended to last a long time. The man is wearing a headband on his forehead, with a jewel in its centre. His cloak is patterned with trefoils (three-leafed shapes). In ancient civilizations such as those in **Mesopotamia** and Egypt, the trefoil symbol was linked with religion and astrology (the study of the stars and their believed effect on human lives).

DETECTIVE WORK

Find out how the priest-king statue was made: http://www.harappa.com/indus/41.html

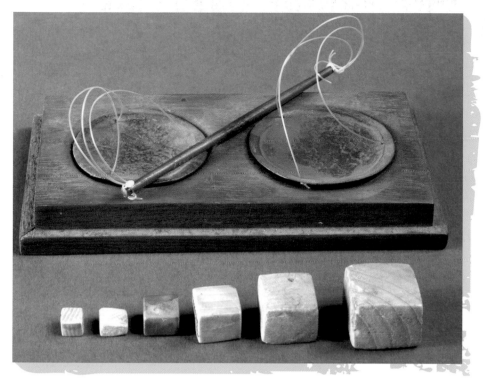

Several sets of weights and scales have been discovered in the Indus Valley. The stone blocks would have been balanced in the copper pans to weigh goods. The wooden base is a modern reconstruction.

Why were weights made from stone rather than clay?

In many ancient civilizations, religious leaders had great power. Archaeologists wondered if the statue might represent a ruler, so they named him the 'priest-king'. We will probably never know for sure, but some archaeologists wonder if 'priest-kings' ruled the valley. If rulers did not build palaces and monuments for themselves, perhaps power was shared out between a group of people, whether they were priests or had other roles.

Whoever was in charge of the valley, they imposed the same rules right across it. As we already know, bricks and seals were the same sizes or dimensions. Every city also used the same units of weight. We know this from the sets of weights that have been found. A shared system of weights would have been essential to make sure materials and foods were traded fairly.

The evidence suggests that the great Indus cities had leaders or officials who oversaw their construction and then kept them running smoothly. These officials must have employed people to do jobs such as unblocking the drains. We can also guess a few things about society in the Indus Valley. Some houses were much larger than others, so we know that certain people, probably merchants, were richer. However, unlike in many parts of the world today, nearly all houses had access to drainage and were close to a well, so perhaps it was quite a fair society.

The archaeologist Dr Jonathan Mark Kenoyer excavates regularly in the Indus Valley. In 1998, he wrote:

'We do not know who the actual rulers of these cities were, but they may have been wealthy merchants, powerful landlords or spiritual leaders.'

WHAT DID CRAFTSPEOPLE MAKE?

Indus Valley archaeologists have found the remains of hundreds of workshops, along with some of the tools used by craftspeople who worked in them. From finds like these, we can tell that common crafts included pottery, jewellery, bead-making and metalworking.

In the cities, different crafts were practised in different neighbourhoods. For example, in Mohenjo-Daro, the pottery workshops were all in one area. We know this from the locations of the many kilns for firing clay objects. Among the common products made by potters were terracotta **figurines**. Hundreds of these statues have been found, ranging from 10 to 30 cm (4–12 in) tall.

A lot of figurines were of women, often naked apart from a headdress, jewellery and belt or short skirt. Many archaeologists believe these figurines are of goddesses and that they were used in worship at household shrines. Other figurines were of men, children and animals, from elephants to turtles. Perhaps these were also used for worship, or maybe they were toys.

Some Indus Valley people were skilled metalworkers. They used bronze, copper, lead, tin, gold and silver to make products such as jewellery and tools, like fish hooks and axe heads. Bead-makers made beads for use in jewellery and accessories, such as belts. Rich people probably wore expensive beads made from gold, silver, ivory or carnelian, while poorer people may have worn clay beads painted to look like gems.

Potters made a wide range of household goods, like this storage pot. Clay pots were 'thrown' on a wheel, as potters do today. They were often painted with simple patterns.

DETECTIVE WORK

It's your turn to be an archaeologist. On this website, you can try to match the broken 'sherds' of pottery to the correct pots: http://www.ancientindia.co.uk/indus/challenge/cha_set.html

Some of the objects made by craftspeople give us an idea of how people spent their spare time. Figurines of girls in dancing poses suggest that people enjoyed dancing. Perhaps they danced to music made by whistles, many of which have been found in the shape of birds. Some people found time to play games, as dice, marbles and board games have been discovered. Other toys, made from terracotta, were probably for young children: miniature bullock carts, wheeled animals (some with nodding heads), rattles, spinning tops and puppets. One figurine shows a boy holding a disc, which looks rather like those used for a game called *pittu* in Pakistan today. In the game, a group of children stack up their discs then attempt to knock all of them down by throwing a ball.

This gold bangle, bead bracelet and button were found in Mohenjo-Daro. They are more than 4,000 years old.

In 1990, the historian Ian McNeil wrote:

'The button, in fact, was originally used more as an ornament than as a fastening, the earliest known being found at Mohenjo-Daro in the Indus Valley. It is made of a curved shell and about 5,000 years old.'

Were Indus Valley board games like any modern games?

The board and pieces for this game were made from clay, with some pieces painted black. The players may have moved their pieces on the throw of a dice.

WHERE DID INDUS VALLEY TRADERS GO?

Trading with other regions gave Indus Valley people a wider range of materials and foods to choose from. It also made some of them rich. Traders travelled more than 2,000 km (1,200 mi) from the valley to Central Asia and Mesopotamia.

No one has found any coins or other tokens that could have been used as money in the Indus Valley. This means that people probably bartered with each other: they exchanged goods for other goods of equal value. When workers cleaned the streets or built a house, they were probably paid with goods such as grain. Indus Valley people traded with each other daily, in markets. They traded food, **raw materials** (such as gold or wood) and finished goods.

Ordinary people probably travelled no farther than the nearest market, but Indus Valley seals have been found as far away as Mesopotamia, so it is likely that some traders made it that far. Journeying long distances would have been slow and dangerous, particularly during the rainy season. When traders made their way overland with heavy goods, they used two-wheeled carts pulled by bullocks. For lighter goods such as gemstones and shells, traders probably loaded up sheep and goats with brimming saddlebags.

The ruler of the Mesopotamian region of Sumer, King Sargon (2334–2279 BCE), talked about the trading ships in the docks of his capital, Agade. Meluhha was the Sumerian name for the Indus Valley:

'The ships from Meluhha, the ships from Magan, the ships from Dilmun he made tie up alongside the quay of Agade.'

Archaeologists base some of their ideas about transport in the Indus Valley on what is used in the region today. This rowing boat is carrying goods in northern India.

The rivers offered an easy means of transporting goods, both down to the Arabian Sea or up into the mountains. Some seals show flat-bottomed rowing boats. For travelling upriver, against the flow, boats such as these may have been equipped with masts and sails. For journeying across the Arabian Sea towards Mesopotamia, merchants probably sailed in boats built from wood or tightly plaited reeds and waterproofed with tar.

In Central Asia, Indus Valley traders bought jade. To the southeast (in modern India), they found violet-coloured amethyst. Just to the north (in modern Afghanistan), they traded for gold, **lapis lazuli** and alabaster. Turquoise came from the west (in modern Iran). Indus Valley towns along the coast supplied shells. Wood, silver and copper were found in the mountains. Indus Valley towns near the coast and on overland routes became trading centres, with large warehouses. They may also have had hotels where traders could rest. Mohenjo-Daro appears to have had at least one such business: a building in the Lower City has rows of rooms with separate bathrooms.

DETECTIVE WORK
Use this website to investigate an Indus Valley model of a bullock cart:
http://www.harappa.com/investigators/cartmanbull.html

The red gemstones in this pendant are carnelian. Carnelian was rare and had to be bought in the regions of modern Afghanistan and India.

Dozens of miniature bullock carts sculpted from clay have been discovered in the Indus Valley. In this one, the trader's cart is loaded with a storage pot.

Do you think this necklace was worn by a rich person or a poor person?

WHAT GODS WERE WORSHIPPED?

Many figurines and seals show people and animals that look as if they might be gods or honoured creatures. This suggests that religion played a large part in Indus Valley people's lives. Water may have been at the heart of that religion.

When archaeologists are lacking information about the Indus Valley, they always look at other civilizations of the period. In Mesopotamia and Egypt, people believed that the gods of the sun, rain and rivers helped the crops to grow and kept people alive. It is likely that Indus Valley people had similar ideas, as their seals and figurines show gods and goddesses who look as if they are linked with **fertility** and nature. These figures are often naked and powerful-looking, and are sometimes surrounded by animals and plants.

One interesting seal found in the valley has been called the 'Pashupati seal'. It shows a male figure wearing a horned headdress, sitting cross-legged and surrounded by animals. Some people think the figure is **meditating** in a **yoga** pose. Others think he looks like the **Hindu** god Pashupati.

DETECTIVE WORK

Discover more about the 'Pashupati seal' on the website of the National Museum of India: http://nationalmuseumindia.gov.in/. You'll find the museum's Indus Valley collection by clicking on 'Pre-History and Archaeology' under the 'Collections' menu.

The 'Pashupati seal' was found in Mohenjo-Daro. Some archaeologists have called the horned human figure 'Pashupati'.

Which animal is shown on the top right of the 'Pashupati seal'?

Hinduism did not fully develop in the region until around 200 BCE, but perhaps it has some roots in the religion of the Indus Valley. Hindus honour cows and bulls, which are frequently seen in Indus Valley art. They also honour certain plants, such as the pipal tree, which is shown on one Indus seal.

Bathing is very important to modern Hindus. It represents **purity**. One of Hinduism's most sacred pilgrimages is to bathe in the River Ganges. Washing seems to have been at the heart of Indus Valley culture: almost every home had a bathroom, at a time when most peoples were probably quite dirty. Perhaps religious ceremonies were based around bathing at public baths such as Mohenjo-Daro's Great Bath. It seems as if large shells might have been used as water scoops during ceremonies.

▲ This modern statue is of Pashupati, who is lord of the animals. Pashupati is an incarnation of the great Hindu god Shiva.

Through most of their civilization, when Indus Valley people died they were buried with their heads pointing to the north and their feet to the south. Their skeletons are wearing jewellery such as shell bangles and carnelian necklaces. In the graves are pottery containers and baskets lined with waterproof bitumen. These containers were probably once filled with food and drink. From this we can tell that Indus Valley people believed in an afterlife and that they wanted to give their loved-ones a good start in it. Towards the end of the civilization, people were **cremated**, as Hindus are today.

◄ Archaeologists think this figurine of a naked woman shows a fertility goddess. Indus Valley people would have hoped for fertility, both for mothers and in the fields.

WHAT WERE HOMES LIKE?

Archaeologists have excavated the remains of hundreds of homes in Indus Valley cities. We can make guesses about how people used their houses from the objects found in particular rooms and from how people in similar climates use their homes today.

Poorer people lived in small one-storey homes, with just one room and usually a separate bathing area. In hot, dry weather, they probably slept on their flat roofs to keep cool. Richer people lived in homes with two floors and several rooms. On the ground floor were the kitchen, bathroom and living areas, all facing on to an open-air courtyard. Some large homes boasted a well in the courtyard. Kitchens had a hearth for cooking. Bathrooms featured what may have been the world's first 'flushing' toilets. Drains connected the bathroom with the street sewer: mess would have been washed away with a few splashes of water. The upper floor, which was reached by brick stairs, was probably for storage and sleeping. A balcony overlooked the central courtyard.

In her book *The Ancient Indus Valley* (2008), archaeologist Jane McIntosh wrote:

'Bones of the domestic dog… have been found in many [Indus Valley] sites, as have a number of dog figurines. These indicate that there were several different breeds, including a squat animal resembling a bulldog and a rangy beast like an Afghan hound… Collars are shown around the necks of some of the figurines…'

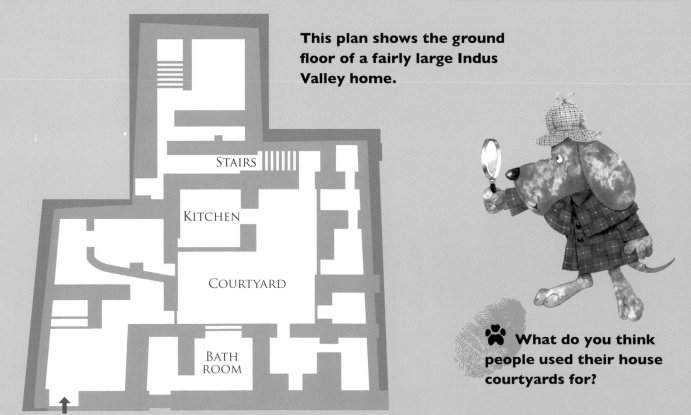

This plan shows the ground floor of a fairly large Indus Valley home.

STAIRS

KITCHEN

COURTYARD

BATH ROOM

ENTRANCE

What do you think people used their house courtyards for?

Dogs may have been kept as pets, as guard dogs, or to help farmers with their work.

House walls were over 1 m (3 ft) thick, which made them sturdy as well as cool in summer. The internal walls were probably plastered with a thin layer of clay that might have been painted. House windows had terracotta bars across them, and perhaps wooden shutters, which would have offered security. There were no windows or doors in the walls beside the main street. This design feature would have given the inhabitants some privacy as well as protection from dust and noise. Many houses had what looks like a bin on their outer wall, beside the road. Perhaps city workers cleared rubbish from these bins.

In other civilizations of the period, men often worked outside the home while women worked at home and took care of children. As well as the many toys found inside houses, archaeologists think that children also had pets to play with. The inhabitants of the Indus Valley were among the first peoples known to keep tame dogs and cats. Birdcages and figurines of caged birds have also been found.

This photo shows the bathroom of a house in the city of Lothal. People stood on the square brick platform to wash themselves with water poured from pots. The dirty water ran down the drain, which is sunk into the ground.

DETECTIVE WORK

Try this website for doing some more research about how people kept themselves clean: http://www.bbc.co.uk/schools/primaryhistory/indus_valley/

Drain

Bathroom

WHAT FOOD DID PEOPLE EAT?

When experts study skeletons found in the Indus Valley, they can tell that people were usually well fed and healthy, although men were sometimes better fed than women. Many other discoveries, from burnt seeds to frying pans, can reveal what people ate and how they ate it.

It is likely that Indus Valley people ate a lot of fish. Archaeologists have unearthed some of the nets and hooks they used to catch river fish. Sea fish were caught along the coast, then dried or salted to preserve them. Bones of sea fish have been found 1,000 km (620 mi) inland at Harappa. Indus Valley people probably also ate plenty of meat. Animal bones in rubbish pits at Harappa tell us that 50 per cent of the animals eaten were cattle, such as cows and buffalo; 20 per cent were sheep; and 5 per cent were goats. The milk of these **domestic** animals would have been drunk and perhaps turned into yoghurt. The remaining 25 per cent of bones belong to wild animals, such as gazelles, wild pigs, rhinoceroses and elephants. They were hunted with spears, arrows and clay slingshots.

On the floors of homes and in rubbish pits, many burnt seeds have been uncovered. These seeds tell us that the most common grains eaten were wheat, barley and millet. Grain could have been made into porridge, sweetened with honey. It was also ground into flour by rubbing it with a rounded stone on top of a flat stone, then baked into bread.

DETECTIVE WORK

Put together a menu for a family in Mohenjo-Daro, using the information about farming and food on this website: http://www.bbc.co.uk/schools/primaryhistory/indus_valley/food_and_farming/

The *Rig Veda* is a collection of hymns composed in India and Pakistan around 1700–1100 BCE, soon after the **decline** of Indus Valley civilization. During this period, cattle were of huge importance. One hymn says:

'The cattle have come and brought good fortune: let them rest in the cow-pen and be happy near us.'

Discoveries such as this terracotta figurine of a bull can tell us about the animals that were common in the Indus Valley.

Side dishes might have been cooked from vegetables and **pulses** such as lentils, chickpeas, peas, okra and gourds. Foods could have been spiced with sesame, capers, ginger, turmeric, cinnamon, coriander and garlic. Metal and pottery cooking pots and frying pans have been unearthed, which tell us that food was roasted, fried or baked. Then it was presented on pottery serving dishes. Refreshing fruits included melons, figs, dates, grapes and apricots.

Farmers planted their crops close to the rivers, where there was a constant supply of water. Some **irrigation** canals, which carried water from the river to fields farther away, have been discovered. Tools used by farmers included ploughs, which may have been pulled by bulls; seed drills, for pushing seeds into the soil; and harrows, for breaking up the soil. We can tell from the seeds found that farmers cultivated their fields twice a year, with some crops harvested in the spring and others in autumn. This meant that fresh food was always available, which was essential in a hot region with no means of refrigeration.

In wealthier homes, metal cooking pots, made of copper or bronze, were used instead of pottery ones.

🐾 **Why was bronze a good material for cooking pots?**

In Pakistan today, green fields still cluster in fertile river valleys.

WHAT DID PEOPLE LOOK LIKE?

Indus Valley figurines and seals can give us some ideas about how people dressed and wore their hair. Skeletons found in the region tell us that people were, on average, around 1.5 to 1.6 m (4 ft 11 in to 5 ft 3 in) tall, which is just a little shorter than average Pakistani and Indian people today.

No clothing from the Indus Valley has survived, but figurines, seals and paintings on pots show us that people were very lightly dressed, as they are in many hot regions today. Workmen probably just wore a loincloth around their waist, made from a looped piece of cloth. Richer men wore cloaks or robes. Many figurines show women going topless, but archaeologists think that in fact women may have worn dresses and wraps to cover themselves.

It is likely that most clothing was made of locally grown cotton, which is ideal for keeping cool. Tools for spinning and weaving cotton have been found in several Indus Valley cities. Leather, flax and wool were probably also used for clothes and accessories. Cloth may have been coloured with natural dyes: red from the roots of madder plants, blue from indigo plants, and orange-yellow from turmeric stems.

DETECTIVE WORK

Find out about a day in the life of a boy living in Mohenjo-Daro: http://www.ancientindia.co.uk/indus/story/sto_set.html. What evidence do you think the storyteller used to write this tale?

This stone head probably broke off a larger sculpture. The man has a shaved upper lip and neatly combed beard. His long hair is plaited and tied into a bun on the back of his head.

Figurines show us that different groups of people may have worn their hair in different styles to show their position. Some figurines of men show them wearing headbands, which might mean they were important. These men generally have beards and wear their long hair in a bun. Other men have their short hair simply parted in the middle. Women seem to have worn their hair in a huge range of styles, from plaits and ringlets to ponytails, sometimes decorated with beads or flowers. Many female figurines have headdresses, often in the shape of fans or cones.

Everyone in the Indus Valley wore jewellery. Men seem to have worn less jewellery than women, usually just one necklace and a bangle. Figurines of women show them wearing countless different items, from earrings, brooches and rings to hairpins and combs. Like many Hindu women today, they often wore dozens of bangles on one arm.

Archaeologists think that Indus Valley people may have used make-up. In Mohenjo-Daro, they have found tiny pots lying next to copper or bronze rods about 10 cm (4 in) long. In similar civilizations, these were used for storing and applying **kohl** eyeliner. Some female figurines have red paint in their hair parting. Perhaps they are shown wearing *sindooram*, a red powder that is sometimes worn in the parting by married Hindu women today.

If you were a wealthy Indus Valley woman, what accessories might you wear?

This female terracotta figurine dates from 2700–2000 BCE. She is wearing a coiled headdress that might have been constructed from cloth or from long hair stretched over a frame. The two dangling side-pieces may represent her hair or flaps of the headdress.

WHAT HAPPENED TO THE INDUS CIVILIZATION?

From around 1900 BCE, people started to move out of the Indus Valley cities. Craftspeople stopped making their finest jewellery, and trade with other regions died away. The Indus Valley script was slowly forgotten. By 1700 BCE, most cities had been abandoned.

Before the cities were finally abandoned, Indus society seems to have become poorer and less organized. Over the hundreds of years that people lived in Indus cities, they did not pull down old buildings when they were damaged but filled them in with soil and built on top. This practice allows us to compare early standards of building with later ones. In the dying days of the civilization, people in Harappa lived in clusters of poor-quality houses among the ruins of the once great city. At Mohenjo-Daro, even the Great Bath was built over. In many cities, the drains became clogged and were left blocked.

So what caused the decline of Indus civilization? One theory is that there was an invasion of **Aryan** tribes. There is evidence of a massacre in Mohenjo-Daro, as thirty-nine bodies were found in the streets and houses. Another idea is that a deadly disease, such as cholera, infected the water supply. The most popular theory is that something happened to the rivers on which the civilization depended. Today, the River Ghaggar-Hakra flows only in the rainy season, so perhaps the eastern cities were abandoned because the river ran too dry. The River Indus itself may have changed course, resulting in flooding or poor water supply for the cities on its banks. Many later houses at Mohenjo-Daro are built on silt, which suggests the city was flooded.

DETECTIVE WORK

If we could decipher the Indus script, we might discover what happened to the Indus Valley civilization. Using the 'Indus dictionary' on this website, have a go at working out what some symbols mean: http://www.harappa.com/script/index.html

Well

House wall

The tall, round structures in this photo are not towers: they are wells. The surrounding homes were built in the early days of Mohenjo-Daro. Hundreds of years later, the wells were dug down from a higher level.

Today the River Indus still floods its banks. In the 2010 floods, thousands of lives were lost, and homes, businesses and roads were destroyed.

The ancient Greek historian Strabo (64/63 BCE–24 CE) wrote about the visit of an earlier historian, Aristobulus (c.375–301 BCE), to the Indus Valley. Aristobulus saw many deserted cities:

'He saw a tract of land deserted which contained more than a thousand cities with their villages, for the Indus, having [moved away from] its proper channel, turned itself into another on the left… so it no longer watered the country on the right…'

The Indus civilization did not disappear completely. Indus Valley people probably moved away to other river valleys, such as the Ganges and Yamuna to the east. They took with them some of their skills, such as how to farm and make simple jewellery like bangles. Today, local farmers still grow many of the same crops as Indus Valley farmers, often using similar methods. Pakistani children play with some of the toys that Indus Valley children enjoyed, while a few of their parents row flat-bottomed boats. Perhaps Hinduism, with its bathing ceremonies, has carried on rituals from the Indus Valley. Although Mohenjo-Daro and Harappa are ruins, the River Indus flows past several of Pakistan's greatest cities, such as Karachi and Hyderabad.

Farmers in modern Pakistan and India sometimes travel in two-wheeled bullock carts like those used over 5,000 years ago.

🐾 **Why do you think that no remains have been found of ancient bullock carts?**

YOUR PROJECT

Now you know about the rise and decline of Indus Valley civilization, it is time to put together your own project. Perhaps you could do some more detective work about the subjects that interest you most. Maybe you could research Mohenjo-Daro and its Great Bath, or find out about who ruled the valley.

If you were interested by the hundreds of terracotta figurines found in the Indus Valley, try making your own. You could mould it from papier-mâché, Play-Doh, air-drying clay or Plasticine. First of all, decide whether you will make a woman, man or child. What clothes will you dress your figure in? Will they wear jewellery or a headdress? What hairstyle will they have? Once you are happy with your design, write about what your figurine could be used for and who it represents.

Another idea for a project is to imagine you are living 4,500 years ago in the city of Mohenjo-Daro or Harappa. Decide who you are and what job you do, then write a diary entry or timeline of a day in your life. Where do you live? What do you eat? Do you attend any ceremonies or important events?

One last idea is to pretend that you are a time-travelling journalist sent back to interview the ruler (or one of the rulers) of the Indus Valley. What questions will you ask them and what might their answers be? Perhaps you could start with: 'How did you become ruler of this great civilization?' Use your imagination, but always back up your ideas with evidence, such as objects and buildings that have been found in the region.

This male figurine has his long hair swept up on top of his head and secured with a headband. He is wearing a necklace or choker. The red lines painted in a V-shape on his chest could represent a robe.

For your diary project, you might pretend you are an Indus Valley potter. This potter in Mehrgarh, Pakistan, is throwing a pot on his wheel, a method used in the region since around 3750 BCE.

Project presentation

- First of all, investigate your subject carefully. Find books to help with your project in the local library and the school library. If you live near a big city, try to visit a museum with a collection of Indus Valley objects.

- There is loads of exciting information about the Indus Valley on the Internet. Make a list of helpful websites: include museum websites, websites about the excavations, and some that give fun details about daily life in the valley.

- You will need to illustrate your project with interesting pictures. Print out photos of Indus Valley objects and excavations that you find on the Internet. Buy postcards from any museums you visit. You could also do drawings of Indus Valley toys or jewellery that you find on websites.

If you are writing about your day in Harappa, you could include a visit to the public baths, which date from 2200–1900 BCE. Poorer people could wash at this public well, which had bathing platforms next to it.

Bathing platform

Well

Drain

GLOSSARY

archaeologist A person who studies history through looking at the remains that people have left behind.

architect A designer who plans buildings.

Aryan Tribes from regions to the northwest of the Indus Valley.

BCE 'Before the Common Era'. Used to signify dates before the birth of Jesus.

bitumen A thick, sticky, waterproof liquid.

Buddhist Dedicated to Buddhism, a religion founded in Asia in the fifth century BCE.

CE 'Common Era'. Used to signify dates since the birth of Jesus.

Citadel A fortress, protected by strong walls.

civilization An organized society.

cremated Burnt to ash.

deciphered Decoded or understood.

decline To decay. A civilization declines when it is past its peak.

domestic Looked after by humans.

engineer A person who uses knowledge of maths and science in building.

excavate To dig up the ground in search of objects and buildings from the past.

fertility Ability to have children or to grow crops.

figurine A small model of a human or animal.

granary A store for grain.

Hindu Belonging to Hinduism, a religion that had grown up in India and Pakistan by 200 BCE.

incarnation A bodily form taken on by a god.

incense A gum or spice that makes a sweet smell when burnt.

irrigation Watering of fields by channelling water along ditches and canals.

kohl A black powder.

lapis lazuli A blue gem.

meditating Calming and emptying the mind.

Mesopotamia A region of southwest Asia, centred on modern-day Iraq.

nutrients Minerals in the soil that are needed for growing healthy crops.

pulses Seeds of certain plants that grow in pods, such as peas.

purity Cleanliness, both of the body and mind.

raw material A material that can be used to make products.

reservoir A tank or lake used for storing water.

river basin An area drained by a river and its tributaries.

seal A piece of carved stone used as a stamp.

sewer A covered drain that carries away waste and water.

silt Earth, sand and other fine matter carried by running water.

tributary A river that flows into a larger river.

yoga Physical and mental exercises to calm the spirit.

ANSWERS

Page 5	This small statue, or figurine, was made from clay then baked in a kiln.
Page 6	An animal that looks rather like a unicorn is seen on 60 per cent of seals.
Page 9	The main streets ran north–south, while narrower alleyways ran east–west.
Page 10	The slabs were like modern manhole covers: they could be lifted when the sewers needed cleaning.
Page 13	Clay is much lighter than stone, so clay weights would have needed to be impractically large. They would also have chipped easily, damaging their accuracy.
Page 15	This board game looks as if it could have been played like modern draughts or chess.
Page 17	Carnelian was not a common material and it had to be transported a long distance. It is likely that only rich people would have been able to afford it.
Page 18	It is an elephant. From left to right, there are also a rhinoceros, buffalo and tiger. Under the stool are two antelopes.
Page 20	Courtyards would have been safe, shady places for children to play and for adults to relax. The remains of tools also tell us that some adults worked in their courtyards.
Page 23	Bronze can be heated to a high temperature without melting or breaking.
Page 25	In this figurine, we can see a necklace, decorated belt and headdress. If you were wealthy, these might have featured precious stones and metals.
Page 27	The carts were made from wood, which often rots quickly away.

FURTHER INFORMATION

Books to read

Indus Valley City (Building History) by Gillian Clements (Franklin Watts, 2008)
The Indus Valley (History Opens Windows) by Jane Shuter (Heinemann Library, 2007)
The Indus Valley Civilization (Step-Up History) by Rhona Dick (Evans, 2006)

Websites

http://www.ancientindia.co.uk
http://www.bbc.co.uk/schools/primaryhistory/indus_valley/
http://www.harappa.com

Note to parents and teachers: Every effort has been made by the publishers to ensure that these websites are suitable for children. However, because of the nature of the Internet, it is impossible to guarantee that the contents of these sites will not be altered. We strongly advise that Internet access is supervised by a responsible adult.

Places to visit

Ashmolean Museum, Oxford, OX1 2PH
British Museum, London, WC1B 3DG
Museum of Archaeology and Anthropology, Cambridge, CB2 3DZ
Victoria and Albert Museum, London, SW7 2RL

INDEX

Numbers in **bold** refer to pictures and captions.

Contents of all the titles in the series: